The LAST EPISTLE of TIGHTROPE TIME

WALTER BORDEN

Foreword by Astrid Brunner

AN NAC ENGLISH THEATRE PRODUCTION

CURATED BY BLACK THEATRE WORKSHOP

NIMBUS
PUBLISHING LTD.
— NIMBUS.CA —

Nimbus Publishing Limited
3660 Strawberry Hill Street, Halifax, NS, B3K 5A9
(902) 455-4286 nimbus.ca

Printed and bound in Canada

NB1712

Design: Jenn Embree
Editor: Marianne Ward
Editor for the press: Angela Mombourquette
Images by HAUI (Howard J Davis)
Rights to reproduce this play in whole or in part, amateur or professional, are retained by the author. Interested persons are requested to contact the author's agent, Gary Goddard Agency: www.ggagency.ca.

Nimbus Publishing is based in Kjipuktuk, Mi'kma'ki, the traditional territory of the Mi'kmaq People.

Library and Archives Canada Cataloguing in Publication

Title: The last epistle of tightrope time / Walter Borden ;
    foreword by Astrid Brunner.
Names: Borden, Walter, 1942- author.
Description: A play.
Identifiers: Canadiana (print) 20230217664 | Canadiana (ebook) 20230217699
    | ISBN 9781774712443 (softcover) | ISBN 9781774712450 (EPUB)
Classification: LCC PS8603.O72 L37 2023 | DDC C812/.6—dc23

Nimbus Publishing acknowledges the financial support for its publishing activities from the Government of Canada, the Canada Council for the Arts, and from the Province of Nova Scotia. We are pleased to work in partnership with the Province of Nova Scotia to develop and promote our creative industries for the benefit of all Nova Scotians.

For my Spirit Guides: Mama and Dad; Uncle Bill, Aunt Goldie, and Cousin Billy; Rocky, Joan, Dennis, Wilma, Marsha, and Brenda.

CONTENTS

DIRECTOR'S COMMENTARY

The *Last Epistle of Tightrope Time* is Walter's letter to the world. The play is based on Walter's life, but rather than a memoir (which looks backward) the epistle is a series of letters that looks forward and illuminate all the possibilities.

The Last Epistle of Tightrope Time is a one-man play, but its vision and scale are more akin to opera. It's a big play and a pluralistic story that is embodied by one actor, who plays ten characters (male and female, divine and mortal, sacred and profane). It's unique in so many ways. The play is semi-autobiographical, but the voices are defined by Walter as "composites of people, hundreds, thousands of people whom I have met over the years."

"We all travel a tightrope to get from where we were to where we want to go," Walter says. "That's the journey of life, and while travelling on that tightrope, all kinds of things can happen…. But even when life knocks you down there is this core or central power source in us that makes us get up, and that's the human spirit. It wants to survive. It's about surviving—traversing that tightrope we all must cross in order to embrace the fact that, in spite of everything, 'we done made it over.' Simply put, it is an illumination of the resiliency of the human spirit."

Walter is an actor, a teacher, a poet, an activist, elder statesman of Canadian theatre, mentor, inspiration, and friend to so many. All his voices are represented and come into play in this text. His story is a vital one, and one that perhaps is best told on the stage.

This is Walter's (almost) final word on life and its divine mystery, but who knows? He might have another epistle for us in years to come, in which case this is the penultimate text from a real leader in Canadian theatre.

Together, we worked closely, diligently, and tenderly to refine and sculpt the text for performance. Taking forty-eight years of material and crafting it into a new version for 2022 was the challenge. Walter wanted a text that not only retained aspects of the earlier versions, but included new writings and new perspectives on life and its journey. To transform hundreds of pages of material to a fulsome but lean text for a ninety-minute performance was no easy task. As Walter says, "It has been like taking a chisel and hammer to a large block of marble to reveal the sculpture already within. Hammering into place and molding the work into shape." Walter has rewritten the play many times over the decades. About this process, he often said, "It took on a life of its own. It dictated when it wanted to rest, when it wanted to be shown, how it wanted to be presented, and where it would morph into something else."

A few days after our last workshop, before rehearsals were to begin, Walter wrote, "Sitting outside on the street patio of Second Cup [in Toronto] trying to let the brain rest awhile. It is such an exhilarating and exhausting time right now charting the path of *The Last Epistle of Tightrope Time*—or rather accommodating the path that it has already dictated. This last sprint to the finish line has propelled me completely into an understanding of what place you occupy in the universe's unfolding as it should and WILL! Where I am right now is a strange place indeed, a solitary place from which I marshal it all to the finish line."

And marshal it to the finish line he did. First in Ottawa, where we rehearsed but were prevented from performing due to the "Freedom Convoy" of February 2022, then fully in production in Halifax the following September, it was a race keeping up with him. But with Walter's spirit there were no alternatives but to move forward dedicated to the stories that needed to be told.

I was honoured to be invited by Walter to direct this production. I am forever grateful for the chance to be moved by his epistle and to walk with him inside of it. I did so in partnership with the formidable designers Andy Moro and Adrienne Danrich O'Neill; I have rarely felt such connection amongst peers, co-conspirators, and guides. And no play would ever have been made without the care and diligent holding of our stage managers, Melissa Rood, Martine Beland, and the incomparable Alison Crosby. It's hard to imagine that any play could be more satisfyingly made. Thank you. It has been an honour.

Peter Hinton-Davis, OC

ABOUT THE PLAY

On August 4, 1974, I sat in a wicker chair in the sunroom at 2764 Windsor Street, Halifax, Nova Scotia, fully committed to writing my memoirs, if you please. Unfortunately, it would take a few more years of living and learning before I gained the insight and the humility to compose and understand the lines that wove themselves into the philosophical fabric of what one day was to become *The Last Epistle of Tightrope Time*:

> pretentiousness will compel you,
> in the springtime of your twenties,
> to think your life an epic for
> a BOOK

My premature indulgence culminated with an eight-line poem and the firm conclusion that I really had nothing else to say. So that took care of the memoirs. That poem exists still in the completed work of *The Last Epistle of Tightrope Time* and therefore truly can be considered its genesis.

The next nine years of writing allowed me to realize two things: (1) the narrative poem was my natural mode of expression; and (2) I preferred to think in operatic terms and therefore fashioned arias and recitatives as opposed to monologues and soliloquies.

In 1983, after reading all that I had written up to that point, I could hear several distinct voices riffing on a theme, as it were, and I wove selected material into the first iteration of *The Last Epistle of Tightrope Time*, a six-character solo performance piece called *Can't Stop Now, Saints Have Trod*, produced and staged by Barry Dunn at the Sir James Dunn Theatre in Halifax.

In 1984, a nine-character second iteration called *Tightrope Time Ain't Nuthin' More Than Some Itty Bitty Madness Between Twilight and Dawn* was produced by the Nova Scotia Drama League, under the auspices of executive director Eva Moore, and staged at the National Multicultural Theatre Festival in St. John's, Newfoundland.

A third, twelve-character iteration with the same name was produced by Tom Regan's UpStart Theatre Company at Cunard Street Theatre in Halifax in 1986. The following year, this same production, co-sponsored by the Nova Scotia Drama League and the Acadia University Theatre Department, Wolfville, Nova Scotia, and directed by Frederick Edell, represented Canada at the International Amateur Theatre Association Festival in Utrecht, the Netherlands. It was subsequently staged at de Engelenbak Theatre, Amsterdam, and then at Centaur Theatre, Montreal, with Black Theatre Workshop as producer. Following this, in 2000, it appeared in print in Volume 1 of the anthology *Testifyin': Contemporary African Canadian Drama*, edited by Djanet Sears and published by Playwrights Canada Press. Then, in 2004, Black Theatre Workshop once again presented this iteration at MAI/Montréal, arts interculturels, directed by ahdri zhina mandiela and performed by Chimwemwe Miller. To date, that is the only time *Tightrope Time* has been performed by an actor other than the playwright. This iteration was published in 2005, again by Playwrights

Canada Press, as *Tightrope Time: Ain't Nuthin' More Than Itty Bitty Madness Between Twilight & Dawn*. Both previous publications are now out of print.

A fourth iteration, facilitated by ahdri zhina mandiela and b current Performing Arts company, evolved in 2010. Some characters disappeared, some morphed into the narrative of other characters, and a new one, Black Man Talking, emerged. Subsequently, in 2012, it was workshopped and presented by Tarragon Theatre with direction by Andrew Moodie, music composed and performed by Adrien Piper-Clarke, and stage management by Jamie Robinson.

In 2016, this fourth iteration, now titled *The Epistle of Tightrope Time*, was produced by San Family Productions Inc. under the direction of Juanita Peters at The Bus Stop Theatre in Halifax, Nova Scotia. The significance of this presentation was the realization that over a span of forty-two years (1974 to 2016), the Host character (the Young Man) had naturally transitioned into Black Man Talking (the Griot) and therefore from that point on had to exist as one of the voices of that character. In traditional African culture, the Griot is the Storyteller, the Keeper of the Record of the village, of the tribe. From a very early age, the Griot's life is dedicated to committing to memory the history and lineage of the people from antiquity to the present, as passed down orally from the current Griot to the child who has been chosen to succeed them. Black Man Talking's journey is one of initiation into that noble calling.

In January of 2022, the fifth and final iteration of the play began rehearsal at the National Arts Centre, Ottawa. Produced by NAC English Theatre and curated by Black Theatre Workshop, it was helmed by Peter Hinton-Davis (director) with Andy Moro (set, costume, lighting, and video designer), Adrienne Danrich-O'Neill (sound designer), Wayne Hawthorne (assistant sound designer), Melissa Rood (stage manager), and Alison Crosby (assistant stage manager). We had made it to the cue-to-cue rehearsal when, because of the trucker protest that crippled the city, production had to be terminated.

The final preparations of the play during its NAC phase were vastly illuminating for me in so many ways, but three revelations were of profound importance. The first was knowing that the completed work should be called *The Last Epistle of Tightrope Time*. I had come to see it as the final testament in an old parchment document that had been compiled by this person named Black Man Talking as a journal of his evolution.

The second was that Carnival Crossroads, a location simply referenced in passing in previous iterations, had been reinterpreted as the critical focal conversion point of the potential life paths we choose to follow, and as such, it is the core around which the play orbits. For that reason, an illustrated map of Carnival Crossroads, along with a brief description of the prevailing conditions that will be encountered on each path, precedes the text of the play and serves to illuminate the heightened function of that locale.

The third, and quite probably most important revelation was the evolution of the Estelusti Spirit, a barely referenced entity in all previous iterations, to the firmly established and essential position of conduit between the Sphinx and Black Man Talking, the Griot. Just as the presence of the Sphinx pays homage to the African ancestry of the playwright, the presence of the Estelusti Spirit pays homage to his Indigenous ancestry. Historically, the name Estelusti was given to the progeny of enslaved Africans and people of the Native American Seminole Nation, hence Seminole Estelusti. When they were forced to migrate from the American South, primarily to Oklahoma, along with the progeny of similar unions between enslaved Africans and people of Cherokee, Chickasaw, Choctaw, and Muscogee (Creek) Nations, the combined group became known as the Black Indians of Oklahoma and was often collectively referred to as the Estelusti. Understandably, and certainly not unexpectedly, unions had probably taken place among the various groups, so the umbrella nomenclature no doubt arose from that circumstance.

In the mid-1700s, a contingent of these people made their way to Nova Scotia, by way of Philadelphia, and eventually settled in Guysborough County. Blacks from the American South had already made their way north and settled in that same area. They had formed unions with people of the Indigenous Mi'kmaq Nation who had been there for millennia. Likewise, the new arrivals eventually formed unions with Blacks and Black Mi'kmaq, and the union between them and the latter group produced the progeny from which the playwright is descended. Thus his homage to his Estelusti Spirit.

Prior to the derailment of the NAC production by the "Freedom Convoy" protest, Neptune Theatre in Halifax had already scheduled it as the inaugural play of its sixtieth season, and so, with feverish replanning and reconfiguring on the part of both parties (the NAC and Neptune), *The Last Epistle of Tightrope Time* premiered at that venue on September 16, 2022, as "a Neptune Theatre presentation of the NAC English Theatre production."

This work was a continuous evolution over a period of forty-eight years during which time no other literary creation was undertaken by the playwright; my living had to fashion the narrative that was the essence of the play—an illumination of the resiliency of the human spirit.

Walter Borden, CM, ONS

FROM *TIGHTROPE TIME* TO *THE LAST EPISTLE OF TIGHTROPE TIME*: THE EPIC JOURNEY OF A MASTER PLAY

SUMMER 1986

Halifax's South End. Rickety house, but not so the people and attitudes then living there: we are white and immeasurably worlds apart from Halifax's North End. Remember "No sex, please; we're British"? Halifax's South End, in the mid-'80s was, "No Blacks, please; we're South End."

That summer, six or seven weeks all told: there is an old, almost antique roll-top desk upstairs in the rickety South End house. Above the desk is a stained glass lamp, by the late Rejene Stowe—it hangs on a chain from the rafters, illuminating the best Selectric typewriter and reams of sheets covered with notes, previous versions of what, by the fall of 1986, was to become the first ever complete version of *Tightrope Time*.

Sitting by the desk, under Rejene's lamp, in front of the Selectric typewriter are myself (white, European, decidedly hetero, orphaned and single-child-chipped by the Second World War—then the latest in wars—Swiss/German speaking, Lutheran-Zwinglian) and Walter Borden (Black, African Canadian, decidedly gay, the middle child of a family of twenty siblings, which included two grandchildren who were raised by Walter's parents as children of their own). Walter is also blue-eyed, Anglophone, Baptist, and oh so gifted. Two more disparate worlds you could not then meet—two cultures, not only made one but, as *The Last Epistle of Tightrope Time* will show thirty-six years later, made universal by Walter's genius, by his fire-and-water-baptized words of truth, his passion for beauty as truth, his commitment to speaking, living beauty into truth. Unflinching, steady commitment to living and to saying out loud. Wisdom in the making.

Not sitting by that roll-top desk in the rickety Halifax South End house was a third *dramatis persona*: the man who did all the photographs of all twelve characters of Walter's play for the first complete, printed, and illustrated version of *Tightrope Time*, the man who was on all the photo sets about town and beyond, wherever and whenever Walter was one of his twelve characters—on Hollis Street; in the backyard of the rickety house (where the makeup for the Minister of Justice is modelled on that of Mephisto in Goethe's *Faust* as portrayed by the great German actor Gustaf Gründgens, brother-in-law to the literary giant Thomas Mann); Prof. and Mrs. Richard Raymond's mansion above the Northwest Arm (for the Minister of the Interior); in Walter's New Glasgow home; at the Cambridge Military Library; at St. George's Round Church (Father Petite's then). I am talking about my friend and husband of forty-three years (from 1976 to his tragic and unacknowledged death in 2019), oceanographer and journalistic photographer Dr. Norval Balch. This essay is dedicated to him.

LATE SUMMER 1986

Norval and I are putting together the September edition of *Callboard*, the quarterly magazine published by the Nova Scotia Drama League. This is the time of Letraset, of cutting and pasting, of typewritten copy and photographs developed in borrowed darkrooms, of newsprint, of trips from Halifax to Kentville to choose the paper colour for the magazine cover (dark blood-red in this case), of talking things over in person with the printer. It is also the time for going over budget without official permission from the NSDL's executive director for the sake of making sure of that rare thing: a true *Lebenswerk*, a Goethe's *Faust*-like life's work, the exchange of life against God (as St-Exupéry has it)—in brief: *Tightrope Time.*

Although my acting "contumacious" resulted in my dismissal after three years as *Callboard*'s editor, I had done what I meant to do: publish this masterpiece of a play in its illustrated entirety. I returned to my work on British playwright Tom Stoppard, and *Tightrope Time* continued on its life journey, voyaging for fully thirty-six years— through the "undiscovered country" whence no traveller returns unwisdomed, the country wherein dwells the Sphinx—toward its final version, *The Last Epistle of Tightrope Time.*

AUGUST AND SEPTEMBER 2022

The play's transformations made manifest and celebrated in the following ways:

- August 3: The Many Faces of Walter Borden, celebration of Walter at New Glasgow Square Theatre, New Glasgow, Nova Scotia

- August 11: a private celebratory dinner, Walter and I, at The Bicycle Thief, Halifax, our alternate space for creative work

- September 9: opening night of *The Last Epistle of Tightrope Time*, Neptune Theatre, Halifax

- September 10: Walter and I on the back deck at rickety South End house, life talks of lifetimes, from *Tightrope Time* to *The Last Epistle of Tightrope Time*

- September 25: closing performance of *The Last Epistle of Tightrope Time* at Neptune Theatre and the dedication of the performers' backstage room at Neptune as the Walter Borden Greenroom

- September 28: my post-run farewell with Walter at The Bicycle Thief

From the play's early version, titled *Tightrope Time Ain't Nuthin' More Than Some Itty Bitty Madness Between Twilight and Dawn*, to its final version, *The Last Epistle of Tightrope Time*, what a Gilgamesh journey, what a sounding of Orpheus's lyre, what an emerging of the Sphinx.

Let us compare 1986 and 2022. *Tightrope Time* is a play in two acts with a disciples' dozen of characters; the first act has nine (The Host, The Old Man, The Minister of Justice, The Minister of Health and Welfare, The Child, The Old Woman, The Pastor, The Minister of Defence, The Minister of the Interior); act two has three (Adie the Hooker, Ethiopia the Drag Queen, Chuck the Hustler). On the surface, we have the established, taken-at-face-value world of act one juxtaposed to the rebellious, forlorn, and uncertain world of act two with its characters of the desert, in which—unnamed, but not un-guessed at—there inhabits the Sphinx. Psychologically, internally, *sub specie aeternitatis*, under the gaze of eternity so to speak, act two is the leavening with which, willy-nilly, the act one characters are infused, disturbed, rocked, changed.

The characters in *The Last Epistle of Tightrope Time* are more complexly woven through the structure of the play, the sequence of their scenes. (Keep in mind that this is a one-man play.) Like Goethe's *Weltgeist*, the World Spirit, they weave in and out, out and in and around each other, into and around each others' thoughts; the *basso continuo* voice of Black Man Talking is there throughout, the main chorus voice assisted and complemented by the Estelusti Spirit and, intangibly present throughout but only emerging toward the grand revelation, the Sphinx. There are five "selves"—at ages five, six, twelve, eighteen, and thirty-two. Black Man Talking and Estelusti Spirit frame the five-, six-, and twelve-year-old selves—Self 12 is also taken into their middle by Mother—and at the farther end are Black Man Talking and The Pastor, each of whom, in turn, forms one side of Self 18, the other being formed by, in order, The Minister of Defence, Black Man Talking, Estelusti Spirit, and The Minister of Justice. These are followed by Adie, Ethiopia, and Chuck on this side of Self 32, who in turn is on either side of the Old Woman. She in turn is on either side of Self 32, weaving dialogue and monologues. Old Woman then bookends Black Man Talking. Finally, Black Man Talking bows Estelusti and Sphinx to Wisdom, whereupon Black Man Talking has the last say. The Benediction is woven of the sum of the fullness of monologues, dialogues, memories of life and lives lived; it is proper Wisdom as Old looks back at Young and, at long last and beyond, embodies and en-spirits ALL.

In conclusion and comparison, *Tightrope Time* is physical, delineated, fast in its Ariel-like movements, changes of costume, lightning light changes, lightning-fast use of the stage, here and there, up and down, in quick precise successions; *The Last Epistle of Tightrope Time* is, on stage, almost static, the quick changes are there, but they are no longer physical, the changes are now soul changes, sea changes more rapid, and a constant *sinfonia concertante*: a quartet, quintet, sextet, septet, octet from the scores of a Mozart opera, where voices voice simultaneously, together yet distinct. This is where the spoken word becomes music. More rapid than the physical changes in *Tightrope Time*, thought, emotion, insight weave into, around, through another insight, and, like "a murmur of bright minutes holding revel between heaven and earth" (John Galsworthy), they make the journey into the interior of the soul. The two plays, the thirty-six years, have become one. The Old Man's question in the original *Tightrope Time*, "What time is it?" is answered again: it is the Time, and it is Time that is not.

JANUARY 2023

In Halifax's South End, the rickety house with the roll-top desk under the stained glass lamp, where the first printed, illustrated version of *Tightrope Time* was typed, photographed, and assembled by hand, is still rickety, the population still mainly white. But now, when Walter comes for a visit on the back deck in the tiny Italianate garden or in the book-filled house, they know who Walter Borden is; many have been to see his *Last Epistle of Tightrope Time* during its 2022, flagship run at Neptune Theatre. They now know who he is, and they revere and welcome him. Walter's New Glasgow, Walter's North End, and Walter as a Black, gay man have brought them wisdom and insights of the kind they never dreamed of.

I look out onto the back deck and into my tiny, tree-filled garden, where small winter-hardy birds frolic and feed on branches and through lattice filigree on this first and rainy day of 2023, and I think of Walter's visits on the back deck last year, of Walter and me sitting there, talking this and that, words and silence, and I smile at how we too, like the rickety house and the tiny Italianate garden in my small and special corner of the South End, have grown eccentric, historical, unique. We are philosophical, a *Lebenswerk*, a *Te Deum* of life and work.

And then I think of one last image, the centrepiece on the stage for *The Last Epistle of Tightrope Time* at Neptune: the toll booth that, in real life, I remember so well, the toll booth on that Halifax parking lot that Walter made his university, reading, writing, listening to opera, reading Dostoevsky, Thomas Mann. And I think of all those amazing people—writers, singers, great and wise and poetic and Black people—that Walter brought into my house and my life in 1986, with *Tightrope Time*.

Dr. Astrid Brunner
the rickety house
South End, Halifax, NS
January 1, 2023

PRODUCTION CREDITS / ACKNOWLEDGEMENTS

...it took a village...

CIRCLE OF ANGELS

Peter Hinton-Davis (director), Adrienne Danrich O'Neill (sound designer and composer), Andy Moro (set, lighting, video, costume designer), Cathy Cochrane (associate costume designer), Wayne Hawthorne (associate sound designer), Melissa Rood (stage manager), Martine Beland (stage manager), Alison Crosby (assistant stage manager)

THE WIND BENEATH OUR WINGS

BLACK THEATRE WORKSHOP
Quincy Armourer (artistic director)

NATIONAL ARTS CENTRE

David Abel (managing director), Rose Ingrid Benjamin (community outreach coordinator), Aimee Bouchard (education coordinator), Stephane Boyer (head technician), Monica Bradford-Lea, Brian Britton (technical director), Michael Calouri (head of properties), Mike D'Amato (director of production), Chad Desjardins, Sean Fitzpatrick, Jillian Keiley (artistic director), Andy Lunney (senior producer), Bridget Mooney (senior marketing manager), Judi Pearl (associate producer), Samira Rose (company manager), Monika Seiler (administrative co-ordinator), Crystal Spicer (technical director), David Strober (head scenic carpenter), Leigh Uttley

NEPTUNE THEATRE

Hilary Avery, Misha Bakshi, Garrett Barker (technical director), Shawn Bisson, Vern Endicott-Blinkhorn (acting head electrician), Evan Brown (head of staging / head stage carpenter), Lisa Bugden (general manager), Sean Burke, Andrew Cull (assistant technical director), Justin Dakai (acting sound co-ordinator), Michael Erwin (production manager), Zach Faye, Kendrick Haunt (dresser), Haui Hinton-Davis (production photographer), Tomas Hiseler (scenic artist), Virg Iredale, Chelsey Jenkins, Hanna Laaksonen (head of properties), Gilann Lafreniere, Heather Lewis, Martin Maunder, Stoo Metz (social media co-ordinator), Nick Murray, Ryan Rafuse, Emily Richards (marketing manager), Nathan Simmons, Jesse Walker, Jeremy Webb (artistic director), June Zinck

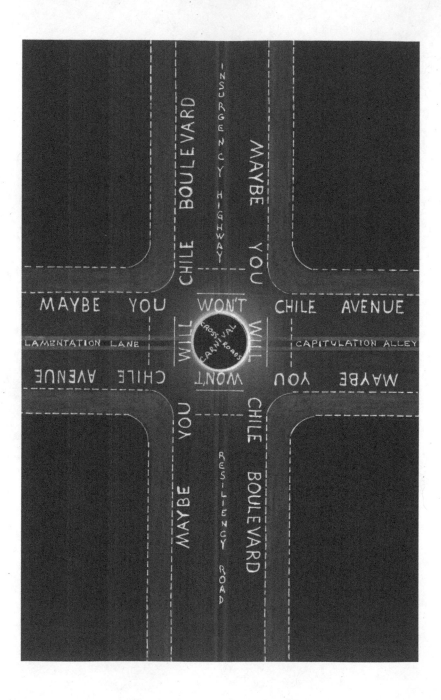

JETTING: CARNIVAL CROSSROADS

AT CARNIVAL CROSSROADS

standing here wondering
which way to go...

MAYBE YOU WILL CHILE BOULEVARD

Route #1   *INSURGENCY HIGHWAY*
motivation: high-flying, adorned
status: living
destiny: driven forward

Route #3   *RESILIENCY ROAD*
motivation: addiction to survival
status: existing
destiny: driven to run on the spot

MAYBE YOU WON'T CHILE AVENUE

Route #2   *LAMENTATION LANE*
motivation: addiction to regret
status: existing
destiny: driven to run in a circle

Route #4   *CAPITULATION ALLEY*
motivation: addiction to despair
status: existing
destiny: driven to remain inert

CHARACTERS

I take my shadow by the hand,
and side by side we walk a midnight mile
together—
moonlighting with a teardrop...
– THE WAY OF THE GRIOT

Black Man Talking: the Griot (the Keeper of the Record)
Estelusti Spirit: the Guide
The Sphinx: the Teacher
and
Shadow Folk of the Village
    Child: the Griot at his earliest age
    Young Man: the Griot as an adolescent
    Mother: a protector
    The Pastor: a proselytizer
    The Minister of Defence: a militant
    Ethiopia: a drag queen
    Adie Day: a lady of the night
    Chuck: a hustler
    Old Woman: a sage

THE LAST
EPISTLE OF
TIGHTROPE
TIME

just arrived
Windward &
The utmost
already been
of May next, at Ashley
NEGRO

MOVEMENT I

Dusk

A PARKING BOOTH /
GATEWAY TO THE UNDERWORLD /
THE CROSSROADS

Black Man Talking enters the underground parking lot along Lamentation Lane. He wears a uniform: cap, jacket, shirt, and tie. He carries a bag of books, a cash box with tickets, a dinner can, and a Tim's coffee. He appears to the world a parking lot attendant. He surveys his booth in the centre of the space and walks a circle around it. He readies himself for his "shift." He flicks on the lights, sets his coffee on the counter, and turns on a transistor radio inside the booth. The strains of Leontyne Price echo through the underground. He listens, then places the cash box on the counter. He hangs his jacket on a hook, picks up his coffee, and stands in the doorway of the booth observing the audience.

BLACK MAN TALKING:
> I want to say a little sumthin'
> to the folks
> of the diaspora,
> a.k.a. The Family...
> we got some business here –
> so, black and brown
> and beige and tan,
> cafe au lait and cocoa,
> dark...light...
> damn near white,
> cinnamon and honey,
> let's head up to the village...

The music shifts and the "village" begins to make itself known around him.

> now don't suck your teeth
> or cut your eyes
> or think I'll disappear –
> jus pick your lips up off the ground
> and give me your attention.
> And don't waste your time or mess around
> tryin' to ignore me –
> I'm in your thoughts...

I'm in your dreams...
we are stuck like white on rice –
I'm the mirror of your inner truth,
you know me well...
I'm YOU!

There is a loud, resounding boom of a drum, a heartbeat.

And I am here to tell you that
♪ *"I woke up this mornin' with my mind"* ♪
and that was an accomplishment
cuz I thought I'd up and lost it –
went and slipped into oblivion
when my last bedraggled nerve was played upon,
and I was sick and tired of...
bein' sick and tired!
Sick of primin' for the marathon –
tired of listenin' for the gun –
sick of knowin' that the race was lost
before it had been run.
Tired of hearin' that my efforts
would *"receive their jus rewards"...*
sick of hearin' that old bullshit
all my life!

Black Man Talking is reflected in the black.

I caught an image of myself
the other night,
and sitting on my shoulders
I saw Reason and Excuse.

Now Excuse was busy painting a big grin
across its face,
while packing a survival kit
to get me through tomorrow:

a bag of *Guilt* –
a pound of *Trust* –
some *Instant Understanding* –
a box of *Turn the Other Cheek* –
and one of *Look the Other Way* –
a package of *Forgiveness* –
and a jar of *That's Reality...*

but Reason said:
"Hey, fool,
I am goin' on vacation –
I am takin' me a rest –
I'm gonna let you ride these rails
all by yourself.
I done tole you now, a million times,
observe a little sumthin'...
take a stand,
speak your speak,
and call it as you see it.
Stop actin' like your will is free
and that you're 'master of your fate' –
your ass is quite securely placed in
lockdown,
while you're convinced you're in
a private suite!"

So I organized my psyche
as I checked out my appearance,
and stepped out my front door
to greet the day –

His reflection fades and we move out into the streets.

and wondered –
how much time would slip on by
before I saw *somebody* choose to stand

instead of sitting next to me
on an overcrowded streetcar,
when the only empty seat was there
beside ME...

before I would dissolve

into a stressed and strained indifference
and tell myself how glad I was
to have that extra space...
but knowing
that's the hurt that always finds
a scapegoat
in the shit that's called
contented discontentment...

before I would explode

into a rage –
and everybody seemed to get an urge
to check their watches,
or rivet their attention
on some fantasized distraction
in the street –
and that included you,
who looked like me
but sat there with a fervent wish
that I would disappear
or that you could change
from ebony to ivory –
and acting all the while that
you didn't have one clue
about my problem,
and that you hadn't just received
the very same reception
that had greeted me.

Well, the answer is –
it took about ten minutes!

I wondered –
how much time would pass
before
a couple of "family folk"
would come amblin' down the street,
all full of *this*
and some of *that*,
with Anglo-Saxon friends in tow,
and spy me with their telescopic vision...
before
they went on
RED ALERT –
and their misplaced
displaced
unplaced self-assurance
tottered like a candlepin
battered by a bowling ball;
before
their heads went spinning round so fast,
they could be actors in *The Exorcist*,
and locked in at an angle
that obscured me from their view;
before
words came flying out their mouths
at twenty-five per second,
and their White friends would just
stare at them
as if they'd up and lost their minds –
which they had;
before
we'd get that game worked out
and agree to "let it slide,"
and they thought they'd made it through...
until they'd gone about a half a block
and ran into
some down-and-out White street guy

scroungin' for some change,
and as they copped an attitude
and looked the other way,
he just up and yelled out
"Fuck yourselves, cheap niggers!"...
and your Gucci briefcase,
        Blackberry disposition –
your Prada-footed,
        Cover Girl pretensions
just melted onto the sidewalk
because you knew
that he had said that same old shit
to everybody else who
looked...like...YOU.

And that's the point –
no matter what the station,
high or low,
to the chickens who come home to roost,
a spade is just a spade
and nuthin' more!

Now by that time
an hour had passed
and I needed to escape,
so I went back home...
and turned on my TV

He returns to the booth and clicks on his TV.

and saw...a sista,
in a twelve-inch skirt,
with her nipples climbin' out her blouse
and her pussy playin' peek-a-boo
with half the nation –
while her Nordic aspirations

fell in wisps across her face
and cascaded in silk tresses down her back –
and she flipped and tossed her head
with such conviction,
that I know she thought that shit was really hers.

And she purred
that she had never known rejection –
could not recall of being 'buked and scorned –
she loved the world
and everybody in it;
and her purpose in her life
was to set a good example for the girls
who might be coming on behind her.

He stands, and as the TV sounds fade, he removes his shirt and tie and places them inside a drawer inside the booth. He's now in a Henley and pants, "at home."

then she went on home, took off that wig,
and threw it in the drawer;
took off those giraffe lashes
and threw them in the drawer;
she took her three-inch, polished nails,
and she threw them in the drawer;
she took her phony titties
and she threw them in the drawer;
she took her padded booty
and she threw it in the drawer;
then she jumped into her bed...
and her man jumped in the drawer –
he knew where all the good stuff was –
and she had up and lost her mind.

He changes channels on the TV.

Then I came across a brutha
as he slouched across the screen
with his thousand dollai sneakers
and a do-rag round his head;
rings and things –
all kinds of bling –
half a dozen diamond studs
sparklin' in his ears;
golden chains, midnight shades,
and a big old silver belt
that fought a losin' battle
to keep his pants up on his ass.
And he struck a pose,
grabbed his crotch,
and barked, "Yo! Litn up!"
Then he monotoned some bullshit
about his bitches and his hos
and asked me fifty times or more,

"Ya know wha'm sayin'?"
"Ya know wha'm sayin'?"
"Ya know wha'm sayin'?"

and I was thinkin', CLOWN,
they got you
on an auction block!

The sound of the gavel, loud and ominous. Black Man Talking stands on an
auction block, dignified yet vulnerable. He speaks his truth.

How the hell am I supposed to know
what you are sayin',
when you don't even know?
And if somehow you do,
then take the time
to learn how you should say it;

and don't be tellin' me,
"Man, you don't know where it's at.
I be talkin' ghetto...."
We both know what's goin' down –
you be talkin' shit.
And somebody ought to tell yourselves
that those bitches and those hos,
who you think are worth your scorn,
are the souls of all our women
who saved us from extinction
while they carried foreign nations
on their backs –
in short,
they toted everybody's shit, including yours,
so the least that you can do
is to give them the RESPECT
that is denied them
by the very ones who pay you
to remain just what they made you –
the very least of all that you could be.
And as I sat and thought about what
some have called
"Our Sad Descent"
from Superman to man,
from Warrior Queens and She-Pharaohs,
Philosophers and Kings...
from Masters of the Intellect –
a people of renown,
I realized
we haven't lost our minds...
our minds have been extorted.
So it's time to file some charges
and make a list of what's gone
MISSING,
if we want to see our house restored to

ORDER
ONCE AGAIN!

There is a need; there is an urgency
for redefining who we are –
        and who we were –
        and who we wish to be –
for knowing what we truly mean
when we are moved to say:
can't pass the buck –
can't mess around –
the journey starts with me!

MOVEMENT II

Charcoal Interlude

A WORLD OF MEMORY

Black Man Talking is sitting on a platform.

BLACK MAN TALKING:
I knew that there was something wrong
the day I watched my living room become
an auction block /
& heard those gentle voices
which had always seemed protective /
suddenly with urgency
& ill-concealed pride
command me to perform /
to earn the admiration
of our poised & honoured guest –
Mrs. Wilson –
who / with due consideration
& unmitigated awe /
bought the goods
& called my honey hair /
     blue eyes /
     & mellow yellow presence
     a WONDERMENT!

I knew that there was something wrong
& ran
& hid
beneath my front porch steps /
till she had gone /
then took my box of crayons
& filled with calm...
     & hate /
I crept up to my bedroom
& hid the brown one
in my dresser drawer /
then I went down to the kitchen
& held the white one in the fire
until it melted all away!

His Estelusti Spirit speaks.

ESTELUSTI SPIRIT:
Poor little sick boy!

A movie projector flicks on, playing newsreels and serial movies from the past.

BLACK MAN TALKING:
Summer Saturday afternoons
are special
for children...
I know they were for me –
no matter what the weekly crime,
the verdict never overruled the mitigating circumstance of
Saturday afternoon
at the movies –
my joy,
my escape!

Ten cents bought a lot
back then,
& ever faithful Saturday put a dime into my right hand
& a nickel in my left, for treats,
& life was complete...

The movies fade.

they say that
children often see most things
out of perspective –
I guess, in ways, that's true...
I can't remember many summer days
that were not sun-drenched –
& ninety...in the shade –
and yet

in countless conversations now
you'll often hear me say:
"What's happened to all those thunderstorms...
when I was young –"

*A huge thunderstorm sweeps the stage. We are on Granddad's verandah and
the road out front.*

death
came riding down the road
beside my home
on a Saturday afternoon...
I was sitting on my granddad's front verandah,
holding on my nickel
& clutching on my dime,
waiting for my cousin Doo
to come running
with his treasure.

I watched a frantic little ant
search diligently for hers,
& naughtily,
but never with a mean
thought
on my mind,
I kept blocking off her path –
& she would run around
in every which direction...
exasperated.

Well, the ant & I
were playing
on each other's frazzled wits,
when a car roared Death's arrival
to claim my playmate
as Its own!

Circus music plays.

my golden private Saturday
dissolved
    into
a grotesque CIRCUS
of broken limbs
    & blood
    & dust
    & shouting, screaming mobs
    & all those same old gossips
      who, like maggots,
      are compelled
      to hone in on a kill,
      & then devour in equal parts
      the horror
      & some tidbits of the latest news...
      stopping every now and then
      to shake their heads
      & moan
      & sob a "my, my, MY, my, my..."

I watched my cousin's mom, Aunt Zonie,
throw herself down on the ground
& I wondered why she kept on laughing
      so high
      so loud
      so long...

& the driver of the car just sat there
on its running board & cried
      & shook...
& I remember how that bothered me
& made me kind of scared –
I had never seen a grown-up man do that...
& the lady who was with him

in the car
didn't seem to pay much mind to anything
at all...
she just seemed to think of
other things;
I could tell by how she stared
         & frowned
         & didn't seem to notice
         what...was...going...on...

The memory fades and Black Man Talking finds himself alone in the underground.

I heard it said
she stared like that
for many, many years.
and deep inside,
with sadness all around,
I really thought that I should feel
a whole lot worse than how I felt
right then –
but somehow it was clear to me
that no one there would ever
understand
those things that now were racing through
my mind...
so –
I simply went back home...

Black Man Talking walks back to the booth, which becomes his mother's kitchen.

& watched my mother
unpack groceries –
they were part of Saturday afternoon...
& on her knees,
among the bags & boxes,

I saw her wipe a tear away
with the corner of her apron.
Something told me I should cry;
so I pressed & rubbed my eyes until
one tiny little drop escaped
& trickled down my cheek...
I tried so hard to make it last,
but it just up and dried away –
I couldn't force out any more,
& really wondered why I should –

so I took an empty mayonnaise jar
and headed for a berry field
across the way –

The sound of cicadas fills the space, and light spreads to a berry field.

not far from home –
leaving at a distance though
the wailing
and the gossiping,
one confused ant,
Saturday groceries,
and the movies...
and Doo—

a grasshopper and I
agreed upon a mutual understanding,
and settled down
to munch away
on a berry-laden patch
together...

MEMORIES!

A symphony of sounds, the field and the distant strains of a female voice sing-
ing the spiritual "Glory, Glory." A world of memory fills the stage.

After-Sunday-Dinner time
hummed
a symphony of sounds
    and smells
and busied itself with
wrapping memories of that weekly family feast,
        when a chicken
        or a roast of beef
        or a dozen stuffed
        and simmering
        glazed pork chops
        slow grooved with
        made-from-scratch brown gravy
        to make a stick-to-your-ribs
        masterpiece delight –
        every time...
        memories of picking berries
        for a suppertime dessert...

    memories of strolling through the graveyard
        for a weekly family visit
        and stopping, without fail,
        to wonder
        how some cryptic, fading numbers
        on a tiny marker here
        or on a tombstone there
        such little space
        to chart a whole life's journey to
            Ancestorhood...

    memories of that hush
        that held our home in its hands
        for just one hour

every Sunday,
when Mama and Dad went into
   their room
for quiet
time...
and nothing much was ever said about it –
that wasn't needed –
it simply...was...
and we just grew into a knowing
and then an understanding
that somehow that one hour kept us safe
throughout the coming week...
and so –
I left them to their quiet time
and went in search of mine –

Black Man Talking sits beneath the "Willow Sisters Three." The sounds of wind in the trees and fishes jumping in the brook at his feet.

across the lane
and through the pasture
where I often shared some confidences
with grasshoppers –
& underneath the Willow Sisters Three
that had wept their shaded counsel
on the bank of a babbling brook
since long before my neighbours had overcome
into a neighbourhood,
I bared my feet
& baptized them in the brook,
then curved my back
into the senior willow's embrace...

I was watching minnows
draw their glinting arcs
against a floral background,

when in a flash, & without warning,
but with cosmic nonchalance,
all that was –
& that had been –
& was yet to be –
suspended
into
NOW

The stage begins to transform with the energy of the Estelusti Spirit.

the fishes & the water,
the willows, air, & i
were swirled into an elemental
oneness...
& all my senses
yielded
to a simple state of
being –
while everything outside of me was reflected
from within –
& for one fleeting second
that stretched into infinity,
i was the source of knowing
that made this manifest –
& my Estelusti Spirit said:

We hear the voice of his Estelusti Spirit.

ESTELUSTI SPIRIT:
You are Nature's Love Child,
a Witness
and a Messenger,
and Freedom is your father –
you were born to be a Griot,
yet you will be called by

many other names –
but Restless is the name we give you,
and you are fashioned from the Wind...
born on some forgotten FRYday
(that's FRYday, with a *Y*;
not FRIday with an *I*);
you are Nature's Love Child,
a Witness
and a Messenger,
and Freedom is your father –
you were born to be a Griot,
yet you will be called by
many other names –

The Spirit vanishes and Black Man Talking is back in the pasture. He heads up to the booth, which is again his mother's kitchen.

BLACK MAN TALKING:
i bolted
back across the pasture
to the safety of my kitchen
& heard my mother say:

Boy, where you been?
You look like you jus seen a ghost –
and you nearly missed your supper.

how could that be?
i sat down by the water
barely twenty minutes gone –
just after two P.M....
& suppertime's at five!

MOVEMENT III

Nightfall

THE TRINITY

The clock in the kitchen chimes five. Black Man Talking finds himself in the underground. Time elongates, stretches, and quells. He takes a sip of water and tries to compose himself.

BLACK MAN TALKING:
    I knew that there was something wrong
    when after I had passed an easy boyhood day,
    & wrapped a hundred secrets in some laughter /
    with my friends /
    I couldn't cross the entrance
    of their after-school meeting place /
    where my "mellow yellow Wonderment"
    might darken up the premises /

Begins to put on black shirt and collar.

    "Oh boy...it doesn't matter /
    you don't need them" /
    that's what people said –
    but yes, i DID /
    & yes it DID /
    it always does...right then /
    but somehow i just moved along...
    although
    i knew that there was something wrong /
    & loathed the way that compliments could flower
    from contempt /

From a distance he hears the sound of a Baptist Church singing in praise, "Highway to Heaven."

    so i became well schooled in that gardening
    and weeded out a method of survival /

He puts on a kente cloth, picks up his "Bible" (The Fire Next Time, by James Baldwin), and becomes The Pastor. The space is transformed into The Pastor's church.

BLACK MAN TALKING:
> never let them see you cry
> just keep them razzle-dazzled...on the fly!

The Pastor steps forward and addresses his congregation.

THE PASTOR:
> You know
> it amazes me –
> it amaaaazes ME
> when I hear the young folks talkin'
> about the confusion
> that's in their heads –
> it amazes me...
>
> and I'm mindful of the many ways in which
> somehow
> we seem to have failed them;
> I'm mindful of the fact
> that we might not have lit the candles
> that they need to find their way;
> and I'm mindful of the fact
> that sometimes we seem to miss the mark
> as we strive to guide them forward
> up to the throne of God...
> that same Great God in whom we find
> no chancy hit or miss –
> because with MY God you HIT your mark...
> there ain't no miss in God –
> God is the Bull's-eye of the Universe!

And I want to say to you here tonight,
though billows ROOOLLL,
He keeps MY soul,
my Heavenly Father watches ovah ME;
and He watches ovah YOU...
He knows where you are –
He SEES what you do –
because my God is watchin'...
ALL the time!

I'm talkin' now to the young man out there
who thinks that he can go out in the world,
do whatever he wants to do,
and no one's gonna raise a hand to stop him;
well you hear me now and you hear me good:
God will stand you toe to toe –
and young man...young man,
your arms are TOO short to box with God!
Can I get an amen on that?

Now my message here today
is taken from a sermon
by one James Weldon Johnson,
in which he tells us
that Jesus spake in a parable,
and He said,

Lights and organ accompany the parable.

"A certain man had two sons."
Jesus didn't give this man a name,
but his name was God Almighty.
Jesus didn't call those sons by name,
but every young man, everywhere,
is one of those two sons.

Well, the younger son went to his father –
went to his father and he said,
"Father, divide up the property
and give me MY portion now!"
And the old father, with tears in his eyes, said,
"Son, don't leave your father's house."
But the boy was stubborn in his head –
he was haughty in his heart –
so he took his share of his father's goods
and he went into a far-off country.

Well, the young man journeyed on his way –
and he said to himself as he travelled along:
"Mm, mm...this sure is an easy road!
Nuthin' like the rough furrows behind my father's plough."

Young man...young man –
smooth and easy is the road
that leads to hell and destruction;
downgrade all the way –
the further you travel, the faster you go;
no need to trudge and toil and sweat,
just slip and slide, and slip and slide,
till you bang up against hell's iron gate!

"On Broadway" by George Benson takes us into Babylon mode.

THE PASTOR:

Well, the younger son kept travellin' along
till at nighttime he came to a city –
and that city was bright in the nighttime like day,
the streets all crowded with people...
brass bands and string bands a-playin',
and everywhere the young man looked

there was laughin' and singin' and dancin'.
And he stopped a passerby and he said:
"Tell me, what city is this?"
And the passerby laughed and he said:
"Don't you know?
This is Babylon! Babylon!
The great great city of Babylon!
Come on, young man, come along with me!"

And the young man went with his new-found friends,
bought himself some fine new clothes –
he spent his days in the drinkin' dens
swallowin' the fires of hell;
and he spent his nights in the gamblin' dens
throwin' dice with the devil for his soul –
and they stripped him of his money –
and they stripped him of his clothes –
and they left him broke and ragged
in the streets of Babylon.
And he went down to feedin' swine,
and he was hungrier than the hogs;

he got down on his belly in the mire and the mud,
and he ate the husks with the hogs;
and not a hog was too low to turn up its nose
at the man in the mire from Babylon.

The music fades and The Pastor addresses his congregation.

Young man, come away from Babylon,
that hell border city of Babylon;
fall down on your knees
and say in your heart,
I will arise and go to my father!
Amen and amen!

Black Man Talking stands. The world of The Pastor falls away. He is back in the underground and sits. The kente cloth falls from his shoulders.

BLACK MAN TALKING:
>I thought a lot
>about that /
>but I knew that there was something wrong
>each time I sat / uneasy /
>in some restaurant /
>& thought about the laws of equal justice
>that with eloquence
>& pomp /
>allowed that I could get a Coke
>but could not rule on attitude /

Black Man Talking picks up the kente cloth and moves back to the booth. He puts the "Bible" down for a moment.

>& there was surely something wrong
>when i was asked to overlook that
>*indiscretion* /
>& meekly be a victim of your rage
>when i refused to take the place you offered me /
>& rather chose to seek
>>& find
>>my own!

With determination, Black Man Talking picks up his "Bible" again and places his cap firmly on his head. The opening of Edwin Starr's "War" blasts from the speakers. He is now The Minister of Defence.

THE MINISTER OF DEFENCE:
>As Minister of Defence,
>I have been taking copious...

yes, copious
and strategic notes,
and I say to you
from the depths of my soul,
BURN THOSE FUCKING CRAYONS!
Burn them all –
black ones...white ones...
red ones and yellow ones,
burn them, I say, burn them!
We can no longer manoeuvre in Romper Rooms...
neither can we pitch camps in playgrounds!
Now git on uppa your thang
an' put some loco in your motion –
git a-steppin' on your good foot
or hobble on your bad one
if you have to –
forget about your groove thang
an' start thinkin' about your move thang –
we are at battle stations,
and I say to you,
I am prepared to lead the troops
right to the gates of Heaven!

The overhead light intensifies to the centre of his war room, the bunker. He gestures a demanding "Stop!"

and when I get to Heaven,
I'm gonna talk about hatin'...
yes...hatin'...

cuz there ain't no percentage
in wastin' love on some damn honky
who cannot stand the thought that
I'm alive

to let him know
he up and died
a long, long time ago –
shoved his passion up Fate's cunt
and got a dose of grief –
now he looks at me with steel-grey eyes
and calls me nigger faggot,
but can't git it through his head
that the only thing worth blowin' is his mind,
and I do that
jus because I AM!

I'm gonna say,
I've no regrets
for tactics I was forced to use
to aid in my survival...
I'm gonna say,
I do not want to hear my life reread
when I know damn well
the parts that tell the real truth
were jotted down in disappearin' ink –
because Heaven's got that all worked out
at coverin' up THOSE scars!

And I'll say this standin' tall
and never on my knees;
the Universe will crack and crumble –
the walls again will tumble –
and the Battle of Jericho
will be a kitten's purr
when likened to the sound of
MY DEFIANCE!
No!...NEVER on my knees!

Defence comes forward and leans on the frame of the door.

I recall how jus the other day,
this white man had the nerve to say to me:
"Sir," he said, "enjoy yourself;
life really is a banquet after all."
Well I looked that fool square in the eye
and calmly said to him,
"How many times have we received an invitation
                    to your banquet,
                    and then were told
                    that we could get our vittles
                    in the kitchen?...
"How many times have we been made to watch you
                    wrap your lips around the giblets of
                    sweet contentment,
                    while we were forced to gnaw the
                        drumsticks of
                    despair?...
"How many times," I challenged him,
                    "will you offer us the chocolate
                    and not the mousse?"...

Well that stupid idiot looked at me
with this Simple Simon grin across his face,
and had the gall to say,
"My goodness, Sir,
you seems somewhat perplexed;
whatever could be the matter?"

"You can take your matters
and you can shove your matters
right on up your ass," I said.

"We will no longer be deceived –
it is the eleventh hour
and the heat is on!
We are prepared to do
whatever we deem necessary to
take our place
at the banquet of life
with the rest of the human family;
we are prepared to fight,
and fight we will!"

Defence resumes his "battle station," and with "War" to underscore, he proclaims his call to arms.

We will fight you—on the street corners
                and in the pool halls;
We will fight you—on the dance floor
                and at the back of the bus;
We will fight you—on the football fields
                and in the taverns;
We will fight!
We will fight you—at the welfare office
                and at bingo;
We will fight you—on the basketball courts
                and in Wakanda...
WE WILL NEVAH SURRENDAH!

Drums. For a moment, Black Man Talking considers the argument of Defence. He removes the cap and let it fall into a box. Everything shifts and bends into the Age of Aquarius—the fifth dimension beckons, "when the moon is in the seventh house."

BLACK MAN TALKING:
Without a doubt
I caught his vibe,
BUT...
Aquarius came dawning
as a Mistress of Illusion,
and she sprinkled crystal promises
of mystic revelations
that reposed in secret splendour
in the Gardens of Delight –
then with tantalizing wistfulness
she crooned a siren lullaby
about a cosmic wonderland
where cotton-candied mushrooms
                        dipped in magic
gently lazed away the hours
watching peppermint-petalled poppies
                        preen
                        seductively
                        row on row
between ice cream castles
        ringed in sunbeams
while cinnamon-scented gurus spoke of
                        Agent Orange
                        and Acid Dreams
                        and told us where
                        the flowers had all gone.
She sighed
beneath the New Age wings
of the Worshippers of Icarus
who shunned our limitation
and soared TOO HIGH
perhaps because
the clouds got in our way,
and while arcing into freefall

we sang a song
of hungry
   sweaty
   summer afternoons
of burning seaside sands
and asphalt anger
that parched their way to
after-hour cool.
When pacified
we watched the neon ripple
           · wink
        and bleed
a cacophony of
emotionless emotion,
the pavement undulate
convulsive liquid seduction,
and grotesque images dine
on macaroni and
   each other.
Then...we...drifted...on
through crooked time,
across elastic space,
where holograms of our reality
showed mountains of defeat
masquerading now as victory
and opportunities long since lost
emerged
to be reclaimed
and vision after vision filtered by
          and vanished into those places
          where lucidity holds its court

Silence.

and for a brief suspended second
etched into the eye of truth,
we glimpsed an image of a picture
of some children
in a lost abandoned kindergarten
trying to spell HELP
with the wrong alphabet blocks

Black Man Talking takes a white crayon from his pocket and holds it out before him, as if over a flame.

and we wondered why we took the fall
without a parachute

He lets the crayon fall.

MOVEMENT IV

Midnight

MADNESS AT CARNIVAL CROSSROADS

Sounds of a loud boom, a heartbeat, now a falling sound, a parachuting jumper freefalling. The sound lands in the parking lot and echoes in the blackness. Black Man Talking hears the voice of the Estelusti Spirit, resonant inside him with bagpipes, Mi'kmaw drums, African kora. A broken clock chimes the hours discordantly.

ESTELUSTI SPIRIT:
> The beaten, broken clock
> > slouched in the corner of your mind
> > is warning you
> > it's way past tightrope time /
> > & its illuminated, amber face
> > > > is not unlike
> > > > the illuminated, amber anger
> > > > that beats a throbbing rhythm
> > > > along the highways
> > > > > & the byways
> > > > > of your mind /

Black Man Talking follows the sound of the voice counter-clockwise to Capitulation Alley.

                now follow me
                        &
                          I
                            will
                                show
                                    you
                                            moving
                                        fingers
                                    that
                              etch
                          a
                  story
            on
              graffiti-laden

                                    walls
                               that
                                    speak
                                         of
                                              loneliness
                                         &
                                    always
                               of
          submission /

Behold Ethiopia!

To the mournful strains of Billie Holiday's "Gloomy Sunday," Ethiopia is revealed standing in her window in a tight white light. In the sky above her, a lunar eclipse.

ETHIOPIA:
an image...
passing as a human being,
contorts a frown into a smile
and telegraphs a message of
how are you?...to my mind...
an image –
pretending to be me,
confuses fact and fiction
by responding with some bullshit
saying,
everything's just great
                    greaaat
                    greaaaat...
that's the sound of a heart
draggin'...into overtime;
the sound of the song
some ancient mattress sings
while whiskey-flavoured promises
are pledged

with panting slur
and climax into
> ♪ *hush a bye*
> *lull a bye*
> *peaceful time is here...*
> *off to bed, sleepyhead,*
> *let... ♪*

emptiness come and creep into
my solitude
and ravish all my dreams
and bittersweet rememberings of
yesterday
when all my thoughts were young
as innocence itself...
and love and understanding flowed from me
like
mann-Ah
> was completely in control...

and *Happy Days*—unsanitized
for early primetime viewing –
meant more than suckin' lollipops
out back
behind some diner;
but no one really thought that we was
fuckin' up TRADITIONNNN,
cuz no one saw no decrease
in the surplus population;
and charcoal grey apologized, discreetly,
for the presence of the colour pink
that brightened up our wardrobes...
then
someone read between the lines of
> ♪ *"Jesus loves me,*
> *this I know,*
> *for the Bible tells me so"* ♪

and found that it was not applicable
to faggots,
according to the Christians;
but not to Dr. Kinsey,
who advised the Church and State
that a capriciousness of Nature
gave approval
to that overzealous stretchin'
of the boundaries of choice
that resulted in libido schizophrenia –
and vindication
tipped its hat to Vaseline –
and all my friends were normalized,
statistically –
and Dr. Kinsey opted for a sex change
and emerged as Dr. RUTH –
and I became a shadow in that

                          s

                              o

                                  l

                                      o

                                          l

                                              a

                                                  n

                                                      d
                          convention deems
                              forbidden...

where the semi-hemi-demi folk,
on one square mile of anguish,
are doomed
to dance
a midnight mass to MADNESS
as it boldly stalks and preys
            upon the hunted;
            and the *hunters* –
            those men

who wander *straight*
into some Pansy Paradise
every evening, after sundown,
where they wrap their guilt in fantasies
of mounting virgin maidens,
cuz everybody knows that *gettin' blown*
don't make you queer
and that's really just benign
          PARTICIPACTION
that seduces homophobia
in all those eager washrooms
where the *Corporate Heads*
          go down
                to meet the public –
and dispenses absolution
          on all those Frantic Fathers
          fingering hypocrisy...CRAZY...
          and someone else's son,
          while *searching* for an *all night store*
          via shortcuts
          through some graveyard
          filled with hearts
          that have no beat,
          but do not rest in peace
          because they're waiting...
          like I am waiting for
          that gentle, elusive touch
          from those to whom
          I anthemed,
          I am WHAT I am –
          I am my own *SPECIAL CREATION...*
so
in my solitude
forever
I exist now as a WHAT
          and never a WHO!

Music shifts to the strains of Dinah Washington's "What a Difference a Day Makes." Ethiopia steps forward suddenly, surprisingly, and pulls on a white fur coat, transforming into Adie Day, a sixty-five-year-old sex worker. She is working the street on Resiliency Road.

ADIE DAY:
　　　　tell me sumthin' sweetness...
　　　　do you know where there's a party goin' on? –
　　　　cuz Adie Day is in a party mood;
　　　　fifty years ago today, I entered the profession
　　　　chile, I stood across the street,
　　　　right there,
　　　　tryin' to make out like I was a virgin
　　　　with a purpose
　　　　if not a meanin' –
　　　　like a rhinestone whore at Tiffany's, dear...
　　　　well, I thought that I would come as close
　　　　to lookin' like the real thing
　　　　till I knew what I was doin'
　　　　in the store.
　　　　Well, honey, let me tell you...
　　　　this car comes drivin' up...

A car horn honks playfully.

　　　　and it wasn't like it is today –
　　　　where every second john you meet
　　　　is jus some fucked-up psycho...
　　　　excuse the language, hon,
　　　　but like they say: express yoself –
　　　　it wasn't like that in them days...
　　　　they made their choice –
　　　　they paid the fee –
　　　　they did the do –
　　　　they went about their business;

everything was copacetic –
weren't no snatchin' pussy on no credit
is all I'm tryin' to tell you.

The car pulls up.

ANYWAY –
this car comes drivin' up,
and this fine young thing
starts givin' me the eye –
well I gets in a panic, dear...
I'm lookin' all around
for someplace else to go,
diggin' in my purse –
actin' like a lunatic...
"Will you get in this car?
I haven't got all night!"
Well, honey, let me tell you,
this chile was so scared to death
I jumped into that car...

Adie gets into the car.

because what was on my mind was
I'd better do this right
I got this poor chile all upset
and we ain't even said hello...
so I'm scrunched all up beside the door –
and john boy don't know what to do –
he tryin' hard to be so nice –
and me?...
I'm clutchin' on my purse
for all I'm worth –
my old fur coat was twisted all around me
so I'm lookin' like a mummy,

and I jus sit there
starin' straight ahead.

Next thing I know
this hand is on my knee
and climbin' up my thigh –
now the only way it got there
was becuz of all that shiverin'
            and that shakin'
            I was doin'...
and baby baby baby!...
his timin' had to be like somethin' else,
becuz he slipped right in
between a shiver and a shake –
but he found that Adie Day was on the case!
I snapped them legs of mine so tight together,
I damn near fractured all of his intentions.
But that was my mistake, my dear;
johnny cakes slammed on the brakes
and flipped me in the air...
I thought I was elastic woman –
legs went flyin' everywhere –
up across the dashboard,
wrapped around the steering wheel –
it was enough to make a Negro woman blush!
So there I was –
all sprawled out
in every which direction –
and...the little train that could,
was a-moanin' and a-groanin',
and you know what I'm thinkin'?...
if it wasn't for that dried up bag
who wouldn't give me welfare,
when I needed some assistance
for my baby and myself,

I wouldn't have to cope
with all this mess –

Adie leaps up and confronts the woman in the welfare office.

oh yes, my dear;
she sat there with her droopy self,
lookin' old as God's great grandmutha,
and said I was a *strumpet!*
Yes, she did!
then she said:
"Most coloured girls I get to see
are a burden on the system,
because they're lacking in integrity...
and instead of doing something useful,
they would rather be a whore."

Honey, honey, honey,
I jus up and lost my mind!
"Look here, Miss CUNT," I said to her—
well we were raised to call our elders
Mister, Mrs., or Miss—
"Look here, Miss CUNT,
since a whore is jus a ho
with a weakness for philanthropy,
I will rid myself of charitable persuasions
while I work this diamond mine
between my thighs,
and that should help keep me off your back."
Well the bitch had made me mad, my dear,
and I didn't have much couth back then...
couldn't fit it in my budget –
but let me tell you loud and plain,
my baby girl made out jus fine;
she's the SUPERVISOR in that office
where I ran into Miss Thang...

an' bless her heart, she shakes her head
an' says, "Oh, Mum, you're so eccentric" –
an' I jus say, "Remember, baby girl,
being an eccentric is jus my way
for changing BLAH into blahNIFICENCE!"
Cuz like I'm fond of sayin',
necessity will kick choice in the ass
twenty-five times a day,
and changes all our preferences into
adjustments!

Back in the car, Adie strikes the john to the side of his head with her shoe.

and a six-inch heel on a platform shoe
adjusted very nicely
to the side of johnny's skull –
so in the end
he bitched a bit...
but he gave me forty dollars –
and forty bucks was MONEY in them days –
then said I was a "lousy fuck"
and kicked my ass politely out the door – Ha!
his viewpoint was undoubtedly
a minority opinion, honey,
expressed while undergoing great duress;
a claim that quite a number of
respected male citizens will support...

Adie gets out of the car, and she is back to her post on the street.

now I'm not sayin' my shit don't stink –
I tote that load like everybody else;
but I jus give a little nod
to the rigours of the job,
then I laugh
an' go easin' down the road.

Don't get me wrong –
don't get me wrong –
there's many a day
when I would love to have a nervous breakdown,
but honey, let me tell you,
my problem is—and I say it plain—
I jus can't take the time.

mm, mm, mm, mm, mm, mm, MM!
tonight I am feelin' HAPPY...
like the woman I was meant to be
and knowed I always was –
oh I might be stalkin' sixty...[aside] five,
an' the legs don't climb the stairs
the way they used to,
BUT THE STUFF IS STILL IN PLACE...
so there's nuthin' much that's blurrin' up
my technicolour outlook!
Two tears in a bucket?...
mutha fuck it!...
that's all I'm gonna say –
you gotta play the hand you're dealt, my dear,
but double-check your hand...
don't mistake a diamond for a heart.

Another car horn and another car pulls up.

Well—there's old Harry comin' now –
with his forty-seven fifty...
two tens
a five
two twos
an' a one –
roll a quarters
roll a dimes
roll a nickels

an' one a pennies –
an' the other two bucks fifty in regrets;
don't ask me why –
come to think, I wouldn't want to know...
jus remember,
you gotta have consistencies in life...

Harry! Harry!
What you doin' up this late?
Hah!...You out to get your batteries recharged!
Well git out here like you got some class –
you talkin' to a lady
who got standards to maintain...
you might be forced
to drop some other virtues,
but never lose the art of bein' gracious.

Adie gets into Harry's car with great style. The Temptations' "Papa Was a Rolling Stone" plays on the car radio.

Thank you, Harry.

An' here's to style and elegance
from the old established school!
There's gonna be some sweet sounds
comin' down
on the night shift.

Adie raises a toast, and she and her car retreat into darkness. Under a lamp-light she turns and loses her coat. Turning back with a purple fedora she transforms into Chuck, a hustler. He is in Lamentation Lane at the corner of Ste. Catherine and McGill in Montreal.

CHUCK:
>People needin' people are a fuck!
>That's what I was thinkin',
>standin' on the corner of
>>Ste. Catherine
>>>&
>>McGill
>watchin' some guy drive
>around the block
>a dozen times
>actin' like he couldn't find the street
>that he was lookin' for –
>dickhead
>didn't seem to know
>there weren't no street names
>printed on my cock –
>
>but what the fuck –
>there wasn't a game I hadn't seen
>a thousand times or more...
>& most of them were just a fuckin' drag;
>but –
>you gotta pay that rent,
>if you're lucky,
>so you deal
>with all the hazards of the job –
>>>like the weather
>>>or no tricks
>>>or those eyes
>>>>that say
>>>>I want to cum
>>>>& love you
>>>>for tonight.

People needin' people are a fuck!
But action's slow
so maybe I'll just give this jerk a break
& he can give me head
& tell his bullshit to his pillow
while I get a little sleep....
Don't get me wrong
the name is Chuck
not free-lunch chump;
I don't fuck for IOUs
            or Mastercard
            or VISA –
just hard cold cash
& services delivered.

So...razzle dazzle! –
there he was beside me
with his head against my shoulder
and his arm across my chest
because his eyes had said

                    I want to cum
                    & love you
                    for tonight –
              & it was minus ten outside –
but who whispers now,
"forget about tonight
& get a little sleep...
we'll make it up tomorrow."

And he went ramblin' on about –
"I know you've had a hell of a day
& you could use some rest right now...
but I just want you to know
that you really did impress me
with how you took care of your friend tonight
without a second thought."

My friend –
who was surfin' on a cot,
just down the hall,
because I saw him freezin'
outside of Britton's all-night food joint,
& I got this one to let him crash here
for the night.
no "double your pleasure
double your fun" bullshit,
just straight up workin'
that "got your back" street code;
& suddenly
I'm Saint Fuckin' Jude,
patron of all hopeless causes...

driftin' off on words
that double-chain themselves into
a doily of deceit

Chuck is spooked.

a what?... where did THAT come from?...

He continues with his trick but is drawn to something/someone in the darkness.

But I let myself feel good, you know?...
a little understood? –
before I got this feeling that
I was stuck –
    rooted –
        in some pool of slime
            & stench
            & sludge –
   statue'd
   ankle deep in shit,
drawn toward
        a sound
        just down the hall...
        a muted moaning
        & some whispers
        in the darkness

Chuck wanders up in the direction of the sound and is lost in the dark. He flicks his Bic lighter.

                        that is Bic'd into a light that floods
            a Sewer
                        that morphs into
            a Crossroad
                        at Ste. Catherine
                                &
                        The Main
                    on Christmas Eve—at five P.M.

Christmas music plays through a tinny speaker at The Crossroads. Chuck is at the corner of Ste. Catherine and The Main.

            & I was trying not to think about
                                back home –
                                down east –
                                & Wise Folk –
            but of
            Mr. Mac,
                        waddling from the West;
                        a blob of dough in faded, natty tweed
                        & knee-high rubber boots,
                        balancing two overstuffed
                                & overused
                                    brown shopping bags –
            an easy thirty bucks...
            & Christmas Dinner for tomorrow
            if I make myself the menu for tonight.
            I know the drill...
            he'll Maybelline my face into
            his vision of erotic beauty,
            & as his crazy, breathless panting
            strangleholds a groan of climax,
            he'll grab his masterpiece in clammy hands

& cheek to cheek,
he'll pose us in a mirror
that will call it as it sees it –
ain't nuthin' but a dough man
& his CLOWN!
DINNER SERVED!
MERRY CHRISTMAS!
BLACKOUT!

Blackout.

then...re-Bic'd

Chuck flicks his Bic and follows once more the moaning and whispering.

& tracking down that moaning
& those whispers –
growing louder...
but it's LIGHTS UP

Lights up. We are suddenly in the Silk Hat Restaurant at a booth with a tabletop jukebox.

down on Granville
in Vancouver
at the Silk Hat
three A.M. –
with a table jukebox tellin' me
I'm leavin' on a jet plane,
while some mescaline,
laced with tranquilizer
made for horses,
keeps reminding me
it won't be no time soon.

Chuck takes a hit of mescaline from a foil wrapper. Worlds collide as the drug takes its effect.

& somewhere
near the crown of what I think is
still my head,
a silver-dollar size of space
remains the only part of me not frozen;

& it registers a flashback
that my friend is now reliving
across from me,
& he's thirteen-year-old Matthew once again...

& on the run –
in search of Oz
& a newly minted Wizard
as a stand-in
for his anthemed childhood Jesus,
who didn't suffer little children
                 if they dared to speak the truth
                 that made them orphans
                 of the freedom that it promised,
but made little children suffer
if they were faggots!

& suddenly
there was Peter,
his saviour & his saint,
bearing gifts
                 of Special K &
                 of Ecstasy &
                     coke...
to manufacture lies

                              that would laugh at Matthew's plea
                              "I want to know what love is, please"...
& with pleasure,
& with pain,
warp him into an emptiness
                              of supplication
                              & of shadows
                              & of secrets
                              & of ways to stay
                                          suspended in a dreamscape...
        the perfect prey
                    for predators
                    & for bidders for his pound of flesh
                    & that of barely turned eleven Jamie...

Chuck transposes to Yorkville in Toronto.

on that night
when they were driven
to a tony part of T-dot,
already blitzed and primed
for all the vultures
                        who were cops
                              & suits
                              & bikers
masquerading now
as good old party joes
                        who laughed
                        & danced
                        & fed them blow
                        until they couldn't stand;
& Jamie just kept sobbing for his
        MOMMY

but they were stripped of all their humanness,
and stripped of all their clothes,
& carried to an underworld to be
the MAIN ATTRACTION
in the Circus Of The Damned
where it's SHOWTIME now

The scene becomes a Jacques Brel carousel at The Crossroads, a circus of the
damned, Montreal, Vancouver, Toronto all at once and together.

in cages –
on fuck horses –
or in shackling chains
suspended from the ceiling –
and there beneath Saint Andrew's crosses,
holding hands, for comfort,
they are swaddled in some slings,
exposed,
& then devoured by the mob –
a frenzied feast
of raped
& burned
& piss drenched, razored flesh,
SUFFER LITTLE CHILDREN!
BLACKOUT!

Blackout. Chuck is lying down in the fetal position. Blackness. He flicks his
Bic.

& I'm back
into my bedroom/sewer
all curled up,
like that baby in *2001: A Space Odyssey...*
in a bubble –
in a playground –

at Carnival Crossroads –
                    spewed once more where
Maybe You Will Chile Boulevard
                    cuts across
Maybe You Won't Chile Avenue
                    alphabetting
                    I hurt...
                    I hurt real bad!
                    I've lost myself.

 Bic out. Darkness.

MOVEMENT V

Dawn

HOMEWARD BOUND

The world is crumbling and sorrowful. Black Man Talking stands with great effort and gathers his strength. He time-travels forward and back to his mother's kitchen in 1974.

BLACK MAN TALKING:
   Oh Mama,
   I feel so old...
   I've seen too much –
   I've felt too much –
   I've lived too much –
   and I'm just feelin'...old.

He walks to the booth in the parking lot and hears a clock ticking and the fire burning and his mother crocheting by the stove.

   The kitchen had that old-time feelin'...
   you know what I mean –
   the closest thing to a womb
   outside the real thing...
   I felt safe.

   My head was resting on my arm,
   which I propped against the warming closet
   of an oil-burning stove,
   with a couple-gallon water tank
   clinging to its side,
   and I thought,
   transition moves with patience and respect
   in my mother's kitchen,
   it knows its place;
   and that's alright...
   makes me feel safe.

   My mother smoothed a doily,
   half-finished on her lap,
   expertly,

casually looped the slender thread
around her nimble fingers
and quickly established an enviable rapport
with her faithful crochet hook.
Old, you say, dear?
No, no, no, I don't think so...
there's lots of things you've yet to see
and lots of folks you're meant to meet
and maybe some more crosses
yet to bear;
but God won't give you
more than you can carry
at one time,
so you will be just fine.
There's still so much
you've yet to learn,
and you're still really just a chile.
Then she punctuated that remark
with a perfect double chain.

My half-cooked egg looked up at me
with a limpid, jaundiced eye,
then spat some fat on my clean white shirt;
I clenched my teeth and groaned OH SHIT!
My mother shifted slightly
                    in her chair,
                    arched a disapproving brow
                    and crocheted
                    in triple time –
the unassuming egg gazed on –
some discontented bacon sizzled,
                    squirmed,
                    and shrivelled,
                    then snuggled closer
                    to the egg –
and I felt safe!

The sun will surely rise, I thought,
and just as surely set,
and in between
I harbour no delusions about the person
I know I am.

The clock stops, the fire stops, his mother stops, time is suspended, Black Man
Talking is in the parking lot underground.

I saw the other day,
on old reliable Facebook,
that at face value at this time
I'm worth about six bucks –
and that's allowing for inflation...
but that's alright by me,
I'd hate to think that I was priced beyond
accessibility.
A second glance reveals, however, a flaw
in pigmentation...
according to the self-appointed arbiters
of such matters...
so there is the possibility
that you might find me somewhere in
a reduced-for-clearance bin.

But if by chance it happens
that you amble by my way,
stop—and have a look;
there are many mansions
in the complex of my mind,
and if it were not so,
I'd be the first to tell you.
So when I say, "Please come on in –
                    put up your feet
                    and rest a little while,"
just take me at my word...

but once inside, please recognize
who is keeper of my castle.

*The clock ticks again, the fire burns again, time resumes in his mother's
kitchen.*

My mother and her crochet hook rested –
the egg benignly indicated
that it knew what I was thinking
and didn't care to care...
the bacon crackled
that it was taking too much heat –
like a lot of us...
a curious fly winged in
for a landing
on my shoulder,
thought about the meal in the pan,
then opted to avoid a closer scrutiny.

My mother dozed –
the hook relaxed –
the egg stared –
the bacon sighed –
the fly performed a manicure –

And I felt safe.

*Time transforms, expands, and passes from inside to outside. Black Man
Talking takes out an old, handmade quilt from a box inside his booth and
shakes it out and spreads it ceremonially on the ground before him. He stands
above it on a dusty brown afternoon road, under a hot sun in the blue Nova
Scotia sky.*

The dusty brown afternoon
dryly said
it had nothing new to offer,

and that pale blue Cyclops seemed content
to beat some heat upon my head with
unrelenting anger;
and so I scuffed along,
stopping for a moment
to pry a pissy little pebble
from between my toes,
where it had found some refuge
after finding easy passage
through my battered
            dejected old sneakers...
and that is when I saw her;
so I ambled nonchalantly
up to her front-porch steps,
where I managed a pathetic,
and not at all convincing:
"Man, it sure is beautiful out here!"

Black Man Talking becomes the Old Woman, sits on the porch in her wicker
rocking chair, and works on the finishing touches of a quilt. She has a conver-
sation with Black Man Talking as a young man.

I know my eyes ain't what they used to be,
but if some MAN was lurkin' here abouts,
I'd be the first to know it;
an' it hot as the hinges of hell out heah –
but yes, I guess it beautiful enuf
for them what got sense to see it.
Now where you from, boy...you from heah?

From over town –
down by the ridge?
It's peaceful out this way;
I thought I'd do some thinkin'.

Then what?

Oh, I don't know...
I really couldn't
say.
I haven't got that
far.

You got some
nerve
to stand in front
a God
an' call that
nonsense
thinkin'!

[*agitated and flippant*] Well you know what they say.

No, I don't!
And who be they and what be what they sayin'?

[*more agitated*] Lots of folks!
They say to just keep lookin'
and I'm bound to find my way!

I don't see how YOU gonna do it
when you can't but read the road signs;
and don't go gettin' uppity with me...
I seen a lot a mawnins,
I seen a lot a nights,
so you jes lissen heah...

seem like everywhere I turn these days,
young folks always tryin' hard
to find out who they is;
most the time they know that stuff already –
they jes wastin' precious time
tryin' to be what otha folks want –

sayin' what some otha folks say –
an' actin' like some otha folks act –
an' that don't make no sense to me
cuz none a THEM ain't acted right in years...

take Bessie Ann...live down the road...
pretty little thing –
from the day that chile come in this worl',
her mutha sayin',
"Bessie this" an' "Bessie that" an'
"I got plans for Bessie Ann";
that poor chile could nevah say her thoughts –
an' 'fore too long
her mutha tellin' me,
"Don't wanna see my Bessie Ann with trash
that's livin' heah;
soon she git her schoolin' done,
she hittin' out this town
an' you can take that to the bank!
Gonna make herself some fine new friends
an' be someone important in this worl'."

Oh yes, my dear...
she stood right there a year ago
with her hands stuck on her hips
an' says to me:
"Well thank the Lawd I got my wish...
Bessie's on her WAY!
Now mark my words,
I see it plain—
Bessie Ann gonna come back big!"

An' that she did...
without a doubt –
eight months big...

an' didn't know what happened
to the daddy.
Well her mutha come a-hootin'
        an' a-bawlin'
        an' a-cryin' –
an' I jes said, "You git on out my face!"
But 'pon my soul,
'fore a week went by
she beat that chile all black an' blue.

One day I'm sittin' on this po'ch
an' I heah this rackit ovah yunda;
I said, Susie gurl, git out this chair,
        git down that road
        an' set them people straight –
        an' don't you waste no time!
Well it musta been a sight, my boy,
for anyone that seen me,
cuz my dress was torn,
my head not combed,
an' my feet was doin' ovahtime –
an' be the time I got down to that house,
I had to sit an' catch my breath –
ole Susie was all done in.
But by an by I gits my wind
an' I hollers for to wake the nation,
"Lottie Mae!
Lottie Mae!
Lottie Mae, gurl, where you at?"

'Twas nuthin' stirin' chile, 'roun that house
but the crickets an' the bees,
so I hobbles up an' looks about
an' drags myself inside...
There's Bessie Ann up by the wall,
holdin' on her stomach
like she totin' 'roun a watermellon –

an' Lottie Mae upstairs somewhere
a-snifflin' an' a-snortin'.
Up I goes!
An' there she was –
all laid out,
lookin' like she jes died...
wailin' like a banshee –
"O Mama, Mama, Mama, Mama!"
I said, "Don't you dare to 'Mama' me,
you ovahgrown heifer;
an' git your ass up off that bed
'fore I slap you 'roun this room!"
"But mama, mama, all my plans...
I had so many dreams –"
"Yes," I said, "I know you did;
but you nevah drempt to let that chile
do dreamin' for herself"...
Remember all the simple things;
jes keep it simple, boy.

WOW!
That's some heavy shit...
excuse me, ma'am,
what I meant to say was *stuff*...
yeah, that's some heavy STUFF;
and I sure do understand
all the...stuff...that you were sayin'.

Boy, save your breath
an' stop right there –
an' remember who you talkin' to;
from where I sit it's plain to see
that you an' understandin'
ain't got no understandin',
so lissen what I'm tellin' you:

ain't no use in cryin', chile,
'bout things that you can't change;
jes stand up straight,
clear your eyes,
an' grab that gravy train
that's goin' somewhere –
there's always one a-waitin'
at some station.

An' don't tell that man
that you can't claim
your point of destination;
you speak right up –
an' say it clear –
determination pay my fare
an' sweet success will greet me by an' by –
an' don't go lookin' mean;
do your thing
but do it clean.

Now, after you've achieved your goal
an' things are lookin' fine,
don't go an' blow the whole damn thing
by sayin' "what is mine, is mine"
an' actin' like you had it all the time...
an' one more thing –
jes because your way was rough
with one ole thing or otha,
ain't no reason why you can't improve things
for anotha.

The sound of a distant train whistle is heard as the Old Woman finishes her
last stitch and bites the thread from the needle. She pins the needle into her
dress and stands looking at her work. Slowly as she speaks, she transforms
into Black Man Talking.

your life is like this patchwork quilt,
where the pieces don't mean nuthin'
when they scattered all about,
but if you take the time to lay them
side by side,
·they got a tale to tell
of who you is...
and who you was...
and who you jus might be –
come time –
but keep in mind,
it's how you weave them pieces
all together that will tell you
if you made a masterpiece,
or if you up and went and made yourself
a mess;
it's the stitchin', not the patches,
                     that completes your handiwork,
and your gumption be the threads
that do the bindin'
on the only windin' sheet
that you will ever wear before your Maker.

We hear the full spiritual of "Glory, Glory" sung deep and low. Black Man Talking, gently and with respect, folds the quilt into quarters and picks it up, as if holding the body of the Old Woman. He offers reverence to her passing and places the quilt in its rightful place in the booth.

Black Man Talking on the doorstep of his parking lot booth. The past, the present, and the future seem to be one.

BLACK MAN TALKING:

We've been wandering here and there
through some chambers in
        the mansions of my mind,
and the journey hasn't always been an easy one –

but...that's how journeys go, by times;
still there's one more stop
that we must make together
before we amble on our way...
I call it my Quiet Corner;
I found it on some FRYday –
that's FRYday with a *Y*,
not FRIday with an *I* –
at half past discontent...
a place where I could drift awhile
and sift awhile
through many moments long ago
forgotten
but that hold within them secrets
telling how we make tomorrows.

And it's in that Quiet Corner,
in the comfort of my solitude
            and the silence of my
                      Secret Night,
that my Estelusti Spirit,
Euro-clad,
undulates in cadence with
            the ceaseless ebb and flow
            of the embryonic Nile –
and She whispers...

*Estelusti Spirit light and the music of the Celtic bagpipes of Nova Scotia,
African kora, kalimba, likembe, mbira, and Mi'kmaw drums under her
whispering.*

ESTELUSTI SPIRIT:
    You were tutored
    in the musings of the Sphinx,
    before She was a virgin in the springtime
                    of Her truth;

before the sages of the ages,
                           revered,
                           but not enlightened,
called Her placid
        passive
        wisdom
        enigmatic
        eccentricity.

The light is magical. From the blackness of the parking lot, the Great Sphinx
appears. The sound of wind blends with the music of the Estelusti Spirit and
transforms in her enigmatic wisdom. She is Africa. Black Man Talking closes
his eyes and receives her teachings, listening with his fingers, touched and
being touched in his griot's eye. He speaks with her gradually, with knowl-
edge, first words, then sentences, then paragraphs, and finally speaking along
with The Sphinx. His face moves from awe and wonder to a smile.

THE SPHINX:
        You must know
                        you are a part of your Creator
                        and the spawn of
                        Perfect Knowledge –
        you hold within you Power
        to create,
        to contemplate,
        but not yet understand The Infinite.
        You exist
                to validate the OMNI-potent
                OMNI-present I AM,
        and yet
        you are not
                without nobility of purpose...
                which is to know
                by re-knowing,
                that you are both the question
                and the answer –

the WHY?
and the WHY!
metamorphosed into
          MYSTERY...
the ALL of what has been and
yet to be –
the SomeThing
and NoThing
which existed...
and will exist –
before and after
the beginning and
the end...
but
YOU ARE NOT in harmony with
THE PULSING of
THE UNIVERSE...
yet
if at times you seem to fail
while ascending mankind's scale,
do not despair –
you are simply less a singer,
          more a song;
          and as such
you are a note of ringing splendour
in the Universal Anthem:
Know Your Sound –
Know Your Sound –
you have a life of many pages
to expand The Book of Ages...
be The Keeper of Your Record.

You must break the ties that bind you
          in a state that yearns for grace;
You must document your journey
          while observing that

pretentiousness will compel you
in the springtime of your twenties,
to think your life an epic for
a BOOK –
but later, as the season waxes
lush into your thirties,
your saga will be captured in
a CHAPTER –
With a honing of perspective
in the summer of your forties,
your story will be written in
a PARAGRAPH –
you will learn to chart your sojourn
as you ponder through your fifties,
in the eloquent simplicity of
a SENTENCE –

but you will come to know
that all you know is nothing,
while cocooning in your sixties,
and your WHO
    and WHAT
    and WHY
    and HOW...
    your ALL...will become
a WORD –
I!

then with wisdom as your mentor,
as you autumn out your seventies,
your adventures will be recounted in
a LOOK –
understanding will render counsel
in the winter of your eighties,
and mould your life experience into
a SMILE –

then in the peace that comes with silence,
and the surety of your nineties,
your inner light will shine
upon the countless revelations
subtly etched in lines and creases
on your face...
and with a deference to enlightenment,
you will simply...drift away... .

*All slowly fades to blackness, silence, and the wind. Even The Sphinx slowly
fades.*

as your midnight offers homage
to your morning,
and your ALL becomes
a single fading sigh
drifting down the corridors
of your dimming consciousness
with this parting truth –

*Black Man Talking is alone in his booth in the underground parking lot. His
words echo in space.*

BLACK MAN TALKING:
You only get from where you are
to where you need to go
by inching on your tightrope,
but rest assured,
your tightrope time ain't nuthin' more
than some itty bitty madness
between your twilight and
your dawn.

Black Man Talking considers it all for a moment. And in the underground parking lot, he leaves his "post." It is dawn.

I *was* born to be a Griot,
and I *have* been called by
Many Other Names –

He picks up the discarded white crayon left on the floor.

but hell –
you don't need to give a heed
to anything i say;
just shrug it off –
plug your ears –
I'm just a
Black man talkin'.

He tosses the crayon to a member of the audience. Blackout. Nina Simone's "Revolution."

END *of* PLAY

Born in New Glasgow, Nova Scotia, Walter Borden, CM, ONS, is an acclaimed and revered actor, activist, poet, teacher, and mentor. As a stage actor he has left his signature imprint in all the major theatres in every province in the country, including five seasons at the Stratford Festival. His artistry has earned him a Merritt Award, a META Award, and a Dora nomination for best performance by an actor, as well as a Quebec Cinema nomination for best performance by an actor in a supporting role in *Gerontophilia*.

Mr. Borden's seminal work, *The Last Epistle of Tightrope Time*, crafted over forty-eight years (1974–2022), with various iterations presented during that time throughout Canada and in Europe, was officially premiered as an NAC English Theatre Production, curated by Black Theatre Workshop, at Neptune Theatre, Halifax, Nova Scotia, on September 16, 2022.

Mr. Borden is the recipient of the Order of Canada, the Order of Nova Scotia, the Queen Elizabeth II Golden, Diamond, and Platinum Jubilee Medals, the prestigious Portia White Prize, the Dr. Martin Luther King Jr. Achievement Award, the Leslie Yeo Prize For Volunteerism, and two honorary doctorates. He is an inductee into the Dr. William P. Oliver Wall of Honour Society at the Black Cultural Centre for Nova Scotia and is the recipient of the Theatre Nova Scotia Legacy Award.